MW00876874

SPEED READING FOR BEGINNERS

How to Read 300%
Faster In 24 Hours

Table of Contents

Introduction .... - 3 -

Chapter 1 – The Basics Of Speed Reading .... - 4 -

Chapter 2 – Preparing For Speed Reading ..... - 13 -

Chapter 3 – Pre-Reading Before Reading .... - 18 -

Chapter 4 – Expand Your Horizons Through Eye Exercises .... - 26 -

Chapter 5 – Stopping Yourself From Saying What You've Read .... - 40 -

Chapter 6 – Limiting Regression With The Use Of Hand Motions .... - 47 -

Conclusion .... - 58 -

Introduction

I want to thank you and congratulate you for downloading the book, *Speed Reading for Beginners: How to Read 300% Faster in 24 Hours.*

This book contains proven steps and strategies on how you can learn to speed read.

Reading is an important skill that you have to develop if you want to communicate with people. Reading is also useful if you want to gain knowledge from books. But did you know that you can still improve your reading skills even if you can already read? This is through the help of speed learning. By learning how to do so, you can communicate better as well as be knowledgeable of more concepts as compared to when you can't read fast.

By reading this book, you will learn methods that you can apply in your reading, and you will eventually learn how to recognize and understand more words in less time.

Thanks again for downloading this book. I hope you enjoy it!

Chapter 1 – The Basics of Speed Reading

Reading is an important skill that everyone has to develop. Known as the "input of information through written materials", reading serves as a means for us to provide an output. Therefore, if you want to produce more output, a substantial amount of input is necessary. This is where the ability to read more materials in less time becomes important.

This chapter will highlight all of the basic information about speed reading.

What is speed reading?

Speed reading can be considered as an "improvement" to conventional reading; this is because individuals can increase the number of words that they can read and understand at any given time.

The advantages of developing speed reading

Although you can accomplish your goal through conventional reading (learning materials), upgrading to speed reading can bring other benefits such as the following:

- It can help you read more materials – a

person who can speed read can cover more material than other people, as they are able to read and understand more than those who are yet to develop this ability. And this becomes useful in situations where you need to extract information from numerous reading materials. Students primarily can benefit from developing this ability, since most of what they need to learn about the field that they want to master can be found in books. This is also true in some professions, especially those that heavily rely on knowledge (such as attorneys or physicians) to do their jobs well.

- Less time is needed for reading – as you are able to read and understand more words than others, you can read all the materials that you have to in less time, and the remaining time can be used on other things. And if ever there are concepts that you need to clarify, you can afford to "slow down" and allot some time to fully grasp such concepts. This can be hard for conventional readers, as they can only process a limited number of words at a time. Worse, they become slower if ever they encounter complex material (taking up more time).

- Speed reading enables you to produce more output – as you are able to read and understand more words, you can also provide more outputs. After all, you cannot produce a convincing and informative output if you lack the information needed in your finished product.

- Speed reading is a better brain exercise – reading is also a form of mental exercise, similar to games such as Sudoku and crossword puzzles. This is because of the process of association (seeing the connection between materials previously and recently learned) made by the brain when we read. But when we speed read, the brain is forced to accommodate more information in less time. Hence, your brain becomes trained to associate faster (as even small pieces of information could make sense for you) and this ultimately leads to better mental faculties such as problem solving and reasoning.

- Speed reading develops your ability to recall information – anyone who can speed read can recall more information. This is because speed reading requires an individual to read in chunks, as opposed to non-speed readers who read one word after another. Those who can read in chunks know how to extract more important information from each group of words that they encounter (as they develop the habit of not reading unimportant words that do not affect the whole meaning of the sentence or phrase). You may remember a few words, but if all of these make sense and are important, then you can recall more information.

- It improves your concentration and discipline – learning how to speed read requires the individual to have a substantial amount of focus and discipline for the task at hand. You can never hope to read more words and understand all of them if you're not concentrating on improving your reading speed and disciplined enough to always practice the skill to get better at it faster.

When should I NOT speed read?

Although many advantages are experienced by people who can speed read, there are specific situations when they don't have to use this skill. Here are some situations and explanations as to when normal reading speed would be beneficial.

- When reading legal documents – if you

ever need to read legal documents such as contracts, you will be better off reading at a slower pace rather than speed reading the document. It may be tempting to speed read such documents because they are usually lengthy, but you cannot always hope to understand what is written in them if you do not spend more time reading them. After all, some words or statements in legal documents are not commonly used in everyday conversations. Also, there are risks involved if you speed read the document and affix your signature to it without really understanding the content. You don't want to be accountable for something that you did not even understand in the first place.

- Literary pieces – literature such as poems and novels (especially classics) also contain words that are not always used daily. Also, literary pieces need to be read thoroughly if you want to better understand the plot or message. Dialogues (for novels) are also important elements that should be read thoroughly rather than for speed, as it makes the whole reading experience more realistic (since you are able to share in the emotion that the character elicits).

- Letters given by significant people in your

life – anything that was written and given to you by significant people in your life such as family or friends are better read at a normal (sometimes, at a slower) pace. This is because emotions cannot be felt when you engage in speed reading. Aside from that, the purpose of reading the letters you get is not to extract information, but rather to feel their affection towards you (which are things that you really want to experience, not just be aware of).

- Instructions – whether you're talking about guidelines for a test or a step-by-step guide on how to assemble objects, you should not speed read any material that instructs you on something. Pictures might be helpful (in case of objects to be assembled) but you might miss some key elements in the manual that can make the assembly easier.

- Difficult materials – there are times when the material that you have to read is just "out of your league". In this context, it makes sense to slow down a bit and read the material slowly or with normal speed.

Myth busting in speed reading

People who've seen others do speed reading might be skeptical as to whether they're really reading; after all, they may look like they're just staring at the page for a couple of seconds or minutes before turning to another page. They may even say that this skill is just a myth, and it is impossible for any one person to understand more than other readers in less time.

This section will disprove two of the most common myths surrounding speed reading. It aims to make you see that speed reading is a real skill that can be developed and give you many benefits.

Slow reading always leads to better comprehension

Some people think that if you read at a slower or at normal speed, you can better understand the material that you're reading because there's more concentration. Although there are certain exemptions to this (see previous section), this is not true in all cases.

What you need to understand is that concentration is not about how intently you read the word; rather, it is about reading at a speed that your brain can handle. This is because concentration is also inhibited if the reading speed is too low (since your concentration is focused on one or a few words rather than concentrating to understand the whole material). This in turn leads to less comprehension.

Speed reading is similar to skipping words

Some people believe that those who can speed read are able to do it because they skip certain words such as articles, prepositions, or other common words. This is due to the belief that they are not important in the sentence. However, this is not true. Speed readers read every word in the material, even these common words. They may not hold any meaning when read alone, but they make sense when combined with other words. In fact, it is these words that truly clarify the meaning of each statement that the reader encounters. This in turn makes it easier for them to see what the essence of each statement is, and moves on so as to understand the next concept.

Slower readers tend to enjoy the material more

Although it was mentioned that it is better to read some materials slowly, it isn't correct to assume that you can't enjoy reading materials when they are read faster. In fact, it may be the opposite (that is, you get to enjoy the material when read faster). This is because when you read faster, the ideas conveyed by the words are also imagined at a faster rate by your brain. It can look like you're watching a television or movie (since the movements and events are moving at a normal or at a fast pace - not in slow motion that slow reading brings).

Now that we've pointed out all the basic information when it comes to speed reading, the following chapters will discuss in detail the different methods that you can use in order to learn the skill.

Chapter 2 – Preparing for Speed Reading

Now that we've highlighted the advantages of developing the skill for speed reading, when it should not be used, and disproved the myths surrounding it, we now focus on discussing the preparations that an aspiring speed reader should engage in to develop the skill.

Here are some of these pre-speed reading rituals that an individual should perform:

Select a practice book

The practice book will be your standard measuring tool and will help you gauge how much you have improved in speed reading. Choose books that are not that complex, such as fiction books that can be used solely for entertainment.

Measure your baseline reading speed or number of words per minute

The purpose of the baseline reading is to help determine if your efforts are producing the desired result when you practice speed reading.

How can this be done?

The following is a step-by-step guide on how you

can measure your reading speed and your words per minute.

1. Use any material (even the practice book) that you can read. Make sure that it has considerable length (more than one thousand words).

2. Time yourself while reading the material, stopping the timer once you've finished reading it.

3. If the time you've spent in reading has extra seconds (for example, 12 minutes and three seconds), convert the extra seconds by dividing them by 60. Add the decimal number to the minute. (Your reading time will now be 12.05 minutes).

4. Now divide the number of words that you read by the time it took you. This will give you the number of words that you can read per minute. In the previous example you would divide 2500 words by 12.05 minutes, meaning that your words per minute would be 208.

Have a clear goal in reading

Are you after the plot of the story? Are you analyzing the character's personality? Or are you looking for important lessons embedded in the material? Whatever it is, you need to be clear what you want to accomplish after reading the material. Having a specific objective when reading helps you focus on meeting it, which in turn helps you to easily find what you need. This is mostly applicable when reading new material (other than the practice book).

Allot time for speed reading

You cannot hope to improve the skill without allotting time for practice. It would be best if you can read in the morning. However, if this is not possible, just make sure that the activity is included in your everyday activity. Even a short 30 minute speed reading practice each day can help you improve and adapt the habit to speed read even when you encounter new material (just always take into consideration if what you're reading is included in the materials that you should not speed read).

Categorize the material between high and low attention

Depending on the content of what you'll be reading, you can categorize it as either needing high attention or low attention. This is where pre-reading becomes useful (more on this topic in the next chapter). Upon distinguishing which material goes to what group, you can then prioritize how you will read the material. Some people prioritize reading high attention first than the other, while some do the opposite. However, it is recommended that you read materials alternately (high-low-high pattern). This is to give time for your brain to recharge after it has finished reading the high attention material.

Remove any distractions

Reading itself requires the person to concentrate on the material. Even if you like reading with the TV on, make sure that there is nothing around you that may cause distraction while you're reading. If the place where you're staying is quite noisy, you can use earplugs to block out the noise. Remember that even a very short distraction can shatter your focus, and it will take you some minutes before you get back on track.

Take a break every once in a while

Take a break when you're exhausted – even a 10-minute break after practicing the skill for some time will help your eyes and brain get refreshed. This is because speed reading involves faster side-to-side eye movement along with faster processing information, which is physically and mentally tiring.

Make it a habit to drink water when you're taking a break. The brain is an organ that's entirely dependent on water for better functioning.

Another thing that you can do while you're on a break is to move around and stretch. It may not be directly related to reading, but physical activity can get rid of drowsiness (a condition commonly experienced by people who are reading).

Exercise your eyes

Speed readers have a wider range of vision than those who don't speed read, and this is thanks to their peripheral vision. This attribute can also be trained by exercising. Some of these exercises will be introduced in another chapter.

Chapter 3 – Pre-reading Before Speed Reading

One of the basic skills that a speed reader has is that they know how to pre-read the material that they need to review before speed reading it. This is because pre-reading can bring many benefits to anyone who needs to read a particular material.

A detailed description of different pre-reading methods will be the highlight of this chapter.

Why do you need to pre-read?

People who pre-read the material get important benefits from the said activity. The benefits are as follows:

- Better comprehension – people who pre-read, especially those who will be reading difficult material, can easily understand the material if they get to read it in passing before they actually speed read. This is because they are able to extract the most essential information from the reading material. Hence, when the time comes for speed reading, they already have the basic idea of what it contains; they'll just need to look for other information that can be added to what they have already learned while pre-reading so as to better understand the concept.

- Faster reading – although people who speed read can read more words than non-speed readers, this can be further improved when you read the material before you speed read. This is because when you pre-read, you already encounter areas that could be difficult for you when you're speed reading (such as encountering jargons or technical terms). This enables you to make the necessary actions (such as researching the meaning of these terms) so that your speed reading is not hindered.

Different methods of pre-reading

Although pre-reading is a generally simple concept to understand and apply, it is still divided into different methods, each having a specific purpose. These methods are skimming, scanning, and previewing.

Skimming

This method is considered a specific form of pre-reading. This is because skimming can be defined as the method of getting the general idea in each specific area in the reading material. If, for example, the book that you need to read is about health, skimming helps you determine that the first chapter is about childhood illnesses, the second chapter is all about viral diseases, and so on.

Tips for effective skimming

The following are tips that you can use to effectively skim the material that you have to read.

- Always read the introductory part – the title and the opening vignette is a good section to start with, as these parts are always direct to the point as to what the reader will expect in the body of the material.

- Subheadings also serve as an introduction, especially if a certain chapter or topic is divided into several paragraphs. Subheadings tell you what a certain paragraph is about even before you start reading it thoroughly. It also shows how each subheading is related to the larger topic.

- Look for unusual words such as technical terms. If you can possibly find the meaning of that word using context clues, that will be better; otherwise, search for its meaning in another source (such as the dictionary) right away. There is a good chance that these terms are important.

- Take note of information presented in outline form or lists of items. This is because these items usually require memorization (another mental ability different from comprehension).

- Superlatives such as best or worst, or information that answers the what, when, where, how, and why questions should also be skimmed.

- Effective skimming requires us to read the first few sentences in every paragraph. This is where the topic sentence is usually located, and this sentence will give us a clearer view of what the whole paragraph is about, as there are instances when subheadings cannot provide us with enough information.

- Always read the last paragraph completely. It serves as a short rundown of everything that was discussed in that section/chapter.

Scanning

Another method of pre-reading that is more specific than skimming is scanning. The aim of this pre-reading method is to look for a single or few pieces of information in the reading material. This simply means that you will not be reading different sections in the material (as opposed to skimming where there are areas that should be read); in fact, your focus is just to find this necessary piece of information and flush away everything that doesn't have anything to do with what you're looking for.

Tips for effective scanning

You can effectively scan the reading material by following these tips:

- Visualize how the information that you're looking for can be presented. You'll be wasting your time looking at chunks of texts if what you're looking for can be found in a diagram or if they're represented as symbols.

- Always say in your mind what you want to search for. This makes you more alert when doing the scan, and you can easily encounter anything that is exactly or close to what you're looking for if it's in your awareness.

- If you need to search for ideas contained in lengthy materials, you can rely on subheadings to easily guide you. As they provide you with a brief idea of what the succeeding paragraphs may contain, you can easily qualify if what you're looking for can be found in that paragraph or not.

- Once you've found the information that you're looking for, it will help to read the sentences that precede or follow the subheadings. This will confirm if that's exactly what you want to find. The material can also provide you with a possible explanation about what you're looking for.

Previewing

Previewing is yet another pre-reading method that people could use if they want to have an idea about the general content of the material. This is especially useful for books or lengthy materials. Unlike skimming, a preview only aims to tell you what the material is all about (i.e. knowing that the contents in the book are all about health).

Previewing strategies

In order to easily do a preview, the following strategies can be used:

- Look for key words – all authors explicitly indicate what their material is all about, as they do not want it to be mistaken for anything else. It also gives the reader an idea about what they can expect to encounter from the material. Most of the key words are usually found in the book/material's meta-description and/or summary. The title of the book or chapter, and even the subheadings are all key words that will guide the reader to know what the whole book contains and help them to specify which section of the book they will look at if ever any specific information will be sought.

- Search for key sentences – almost all materials have a key sentence (also known as a topic sentence). And since all materials are written with a certain structure, locating the key sentences is not that difficult. If the material is divided into several paragraphs or subheadings, you can expect a different key sentence for each paragraph. Also, the most important information in any subheading or paragraph is always located at the beginning (as it focuses our attention on what to expect in that section). The last section, on the other hand, is a summary of the whole paragraph (and is important in recalling the important points discussed in it).

- Numbers or names, pictures or graphs, and other formats in the text such as underlining, italics, or quotes are also significant information that should be looked at when previewing.

Pre-reading is similar to surveying, in that it helps you to determine which areas are important and need attention. By being familiar with the material that you'll be dealing with, it will be easier for you to understand the material even before you start reading, which will prevent your reading speed from being slowed down. It will also help you find the material that you are looking for in less time. Pre-reading and speed reading combined will ultimately increase the number of words that you can read in a shorter amount of time.

Chapter 4 – Expand your horizons through eye exercises

Reading is an activity that uses the eyes. This simply means that if anyone wants to develop speed reading, they need to start training their eyes so that they can recognize more words.

This chapter will focus on basic exercises that you can use to improve the scope of your eyes.

Peripheral vision

Peripheral vision refers to the field that can be recognized by your eyes beyond what you're looking at directly. Although we usually fix our sight on what's in front of us, we can still have an idea of what's happening in the area outside of our focus – that is our peripheral vision.

In most cases, we tend to only focus on a single or a few objects – applied in reading, this simply means that we only concentrate on a few words and do not recognize the rest until we fix our attention to them. By developing our peripheral vision in reading, we get to widen the horizontal scope of our eyes so that our focus also widens. This will ultimately lead to recognizing more words and therefore, faster reading speed.

Peripheral vision exercises

This section will introduce some basic exercises that can be used to improve peripheral vision, so you can read faster.

Side to side thumb exercise

1. Start by straightening the focus of your vision. Maintain the proper posture while doing this exercise (sitting or standing straight also helps combat sleepiness, as slouching can make you too relaxed).

2. Hold your thumbs up while you slowly stretch your arms to the side. Stop stretching once your arms are level with your shoulders.

3. While in this pose, try to glance at either one of your arms (any direction is fine) and try to see if you can see your thumb. It's perfectly fine if you can't see it at first.

4. Glance at the other side, and repeat this at least ten to twelve times. This will be one set of exercises. Do at least three sets every day.

The purpose of this exercise is to stretch the muscles in your eyes, and ultimately increase their capacity to read more words.

Stimulus recognition exercise

Another exercise similar to the first requires you to have a partner and some materials. Here is the exercise's step-by-step procedure:

1. Ask your partner to get hold of any stimulus card or object that can be used for the exercise (such as a card with color, word, or number).

2. Ask them to stand on either your left or right side, maintaining an arm's distance from you.

3. Once they're in position, they will start showing the stimulus object. Your job is to recognize what is shown in it. Your partner can record your progress, and then shift on the opposite side for the same exercise (although with a different stimulus object).

4. If you can find one more person, this exercise can be done alternately, with the one side flashing first followed by the other side. You can also add time pressure so that it becomes more exciting.

The concept of this exercise is similar to the first, but made to look like a game or contest. It also trains your eyes to shift from left to right rapidly, which mimics the motion used by the eyes when reading.

Eye writing exercise

Here is the step-by-step guide on how to properly do eye writing.

1. Look at a wall that is located far from you.

2. Once you're staring at the wall, imagine that you'll be writing your name or any word. Use your eyes to mimic your hand movement if ever you'll be writing it.

The aim of this exercise is for your eyes to have a wider and farther vision (as you'll be focusing on an object that's far from you). Another benefit that this exercise gives is that it stretches the muscles of your eyes while you maintain your head in the same position (only the eyes will be moving to mimic the motion of writing the word), with the movement you're making not limited horizontally (as there are instances when you need to write a circularly or vertically).

Yoga pose eye exercise

Yet another exercise to help develop your peripheral vision involves you maintaining a yoga pose while stretching your eye muscles left and right. And the best part in this exercise is that it is difficult to cheat while doing it; this is because if you did, there's a great tendency that you'll lose your balance (forcing you to repeat it).

The following is a step-by-step guide on how you can execute this exercise properly.

1. As a safety measure, make sure that you're standing next to an object that you can hold on to if ever you lose your balance. A sturdy table or chair is the preferred object. Don't stand close to a wall.

2. Stand straight and make sure that your feet are somehow aligned with your shoulders.

3. With your head also straight, look at an object that's at least 9 to 10 feet away from the front of your nose (make an estimate as to what object is aligned with your nose and look at it).

4. Bring your palms together (like you're praying) and place them in front of your chest.

5. While still in balance, slowly raise either of your feet (whichever foot you're comfortable with) until it is knee high. For a more difficult pose, you can place the raised foot on the inner thigh of your other foot.

6. Still maintaining your head's position, try to glance as far as you can in one direction. Focus on the farthest object that you can see in that direction before you shift on

the other side. Make sure that you don't move your head; doing so will cause you to lose balance (hence, you only rely on the power of your eye muscles to recognize the object on that side).

7. Do step 6 for at least 30 seconds before you slowly bring down the elevated foot.

8. Do the same steps for the opposite foot. Balancing both the left and right foot is considered one set. Do three sets.

This exercise doubles as a physical activity, which is useful if you want to take a stretch after reading for quite some time. It helps to re-focus your brain since it helps combat drowsiness.

Changing distances exercise

Aside from training your eyes to become flexible and be able to see more things even when they're stretched in extreme directions, another important attribute in the eyes that you should work on is the ciliary muscle. This is the one responsible for our lens (which is the area that expands or constricts depending on the distance of the object). This is also important in peripheral vision because if our eyes find it difficult to see objects when viewed from afar, it can also be difficult for us to focus on more words (as it will be easier for us to look at few words). This exercise will help train our ciliary muscles and further enhance the ability of your eyes.

1. Hold your finger or any small-sized object at least 6 inches away from the front of your nose. Focus on the object for around 5 to 10 seconds, or until you're able to see it clearly.

2. Once you've focused clearly on that object, slowly look at an object that is located at least 9 to 10 feet in front of you. Divert your focus on the farther object for some seconds, or until you can see it clearly.

3. Shift back your focus on the closer object. Repeat this exercise at least ten times.

You know that you're doing the exercise right when everything else aside from the object that you're focusing on becomes blurred. This exercise is mostly recommended for readers who reached the age of 40. Research shows that it is at this age that the person's ciliary muscles start to deteriorate.

Another version of this exercise involves taking a 10-second break after reading for 10 straight minutes and stare at an object that is 10 feet away from you until you see it clearly. After this, you continue reading and repeat the exercise after another 10 minutes. This is an actual exercise that you can apply while you read, allowing you to extract information from the material and at the same time strengthen your ciliary muscles.

All-direction computer-aided eye exercise

The following is the step-by-step guide on how this exercise can be done properly:

1. Use a computer program (such as a movie maker or application used for presentations such as PowerPoint) for the exercise. Make sure that the program has an animation feature such as blink.

2. Write 4 different letters, numbers, or any symbol on all sides of the page.

3. Once the symbols are written, apply the blinking animation on them. Make sure that the timeline for blinking will be for two numbers at any given time, and it should change after a set interval.

4. Example:

5. You will write the numbers 1 and 2 on the upper left and right corners respectively, followed by the numbers 3 and 4 on the lower left and right corners. Make them blink by pairs (1 and 2 should blink one after another, with 3 and 4 hidden not to be seen), utilizing either horizontal, vertical (1 and 3, or 2 and 4), and diagonal (1 and

4, or 2 and 3). The timing is entirely up to you.

6. View the animated text, making sure that your eyes follow the movement made by the animation effect.

Just as with the previous eye exercises, this aims to improve your eye muscles and enable them to easily move in almost all directions. Although the motion that is mostly used in reading is horizontal, you will see that this exercise can be beneficial once the method of using finger motion to speed up reading is introduced (this topic will be further discussed in another chapter).

Rapid series visual presentation

The Rapid Series Visual Presentation (RSVP) started as an experiment to increase the individual's level of attention. But applying this exercise can also enhance the reading speed of the person. This is because the proponents of this idea believe that if a person can reduce their "attentional blink", they are able to notice more things (which is similar to widening one's scope).

How does it work?

This exercise involves the use of a computer, wherein you are asked to recognize the word that is formed or specific letters or numbers that you should find while the message is blinking.

Example: You want to find the numbers 6, 1, and 9 on the sequence 61N9eR. Applying this sequence in the program, it will then flash each character one by one, but there's a very short interval between each letter. Once it finishes flashing the characters, the person will then be asked the position of the stimulus in the sequence. There is only a few milliseconds of an interval before the next character is flashed, making it very hard to recognize; simply put, you only get to see the whole sequence in less than a second.

The purpose of this activity is to train the person into becoming more attentive for a longer period of time, with their attention not taking a break even if the first stimuli that should be looked for was already found. The increase in attention can ultimately lead to faster reading, as those who want to push themselves to read faster will eventually need to pay more attention to what they're seeing - or else, they risk losing everything they've learned and losing their place in the material.

Chunk reading

Aside from widening the scope of your vision, another method that can be used to strengthen your eyes and make speed reading possible is learning how to read groups of words, also referred to as chunking.

The usual pattern of reading practiced by most people involves giving attention to one word first before moving to the next. In chunk reading, the person learns to read groups of words. Not only will it save time, it also gives them the benefit of easily understanding what they're reading. After all, a combination of words makes more sense than any single word.

With continuous practice in chunk reading, you can become familiar with more word groups that are commonly used in sentences. This is an advantage, as you will spend less time reading these word groups and move on to the next word group.

How can you develop this skill?

The following tips will guide you in learning how to chunk read:

1. Find any material that is interesting for you. Even a short article will work fine.

2. Start reading the material. However, when you do so, make sure that your attention is on two words, not just one. This strategy is used by people who are just beginning with chunking, and is done so that your

brain will get used to attending to two words once it sees reading material. Eventually, your ability to read groups of words will improve. With continuous practice, you can learn to recognize even four to five words simultaneously.

3. Use a pointer while reading. This will guide you as to what words you should be reading. If you're reading two words at the same time, the pointer should be at the second word. You can use a pen or your fingers to point to the word. For reading devices such as computers or tablets, you can use the mouse, highlighters, or other built-in devices (some of the modern reading gadgets have these devices).

4. Start reading in the middle of the phrase. The purpose of this is to train your eyes and to develop your peripheral vision, as you will learn how to read words before and after the target phrase. This is usually started once you start reading three words at the same time.

5. Practice should be limited to around 10 to 15 minutes at least three times a day. This is because chunk reading demands attention and conscious effort to break your old habit of reading one word at a time, which can be mentally exhausting. It

may cause your brain to become tired, and your reading speed may be affected once you start your speed reading process.

Chunk reading exercises

Aside from the guidelines that you need to observe to learn this skill, you can also use the following exercises so as to make learning faster:

Arranging the material into word groups with the help of your computer

If you're reading materials that are saved on your computer, you can learn chunk reading faster by arranging the text into meaningful word groups. Just like how a haiku has a determined number of words, you can use the office applications to edit the material and customize it based on how many words in a group you want to read. Consider this example:

If you <u>will</u> be arranging

Your reading <u>material</u> into meaningful

Word groups, <u>this</u> is how

The finished <u>product</u> looks like.

This explains why poems can be read easily, no matter how long they can be. This is also good training so that your eyes will always look at a specific number of words while reading.

Underlining middle words

Aside from arranging the material into meaningful word groups, you can also apply your skill in peripheral vision by starting to read in the middle of that word group.

In the example presented above, you can observe that there are underlined words. This will be the visual guide that you will need so that you can focus your gaze on the middle word, and eventually extend your peripheral vision to read the words on both sides. As the word has a different formatting, your eyes will surely notice the underlined word and focus on reading it first. You can use this to your advantage and practice to start reading on the middle part of the word group. As you continue to develop both of these skills, you will then be able to read in chunks even without the arrangement and formatting of the material.

Both of these methods are useful in developing your scope in reading. Peripheral vision exercise enables you to clearly see words on the periphery and trains your eyes so they can move faster from one side to another. Chunk reading enables you to focus your attention to more than one word and understand these groups of words. These are good exercises for your eyes so that they become more prepared for speed reading.

Chapter 5 – Stopping Yourself From Saying What You've Read

In the previous chapters, the discussion revolves around getting prepared for speed reading. This involves setting the standard for a speed reading practice and highlighting how some skills should be developed so that learning how to speed read will be easier. In this chapter though, we will focus on solving a problem area that causes many people's reading speed to suffer: sub-vocalization.

What is sub-vocalization?

Just as what the chapter title indicates, this is the habit of pronouncing what you are reading – regardless of whether you say the word out loud, pronounce it at a volume that only you can hear, or say each word that you encounter in your mind.

What contributes to this habit?

- The following could explain why people develop this habit:

- It reduces re-reading – some people believe that for them to understand what they're reading right away and avoid reading it again, the only way is to attend to every word written in the material. By doing so, they can decode its meaning at that exact moment and avoid going back to it after they've read the material. This then leads the person to progress slowly in their reading, and is similar to the belief that slow reading is equivalent to better comprehension (see section about speed reading myths).

- Most people believe that words are everything in the material, and each of them is essential to give you more details. However, what's more important is the meaning that the combination of words carries, not what each single word carries. It would be very hard to extract the main idea of the material if you over-analyze the meaning of each word and put them together. This problem can be countered if the individual has developed his/her peripheral vision and learned how to read in chunks (see previous chapter).

- This habit was adapted because most people were taught to read aloud each word when they're just beginning to learn how to read. This is also the easiest method to learn the word's pronunciation as well as to develop the ability of the child to speak.

How to minimize sub-vocalization

Solving the problem of sub-vocalization can be hard. After all, most people find this system to be working for them since they've learned how to read (they are still able to comprehend the meaning of materials even if they don't speed read). However, the practice of such is a big obstacle that inhibits the person's ability to read more words in less time. And if you want to develop the skill of reading faster, you will need to minimize this habit as early as possible.

The following tips can guide you as to what can be done to remove this habit and speed up your reading:

- Make reading challenging – one exercise that you can use to eliminate sub-vocalization is to challenge yourself while you read the material. Since you want to increase the number of words that you can read, you can time yourself while you read and record the number of words that you're able to read in the given time. By doing so, you'll be more exposed to reading through the meaning of the words – not just the single word – so that you can beat your record for each reading session. This becomes more possible if you're able to develop the skills mentioned earlier in this book (most specifically, learning how to read chunks of words).

- Distract your mind by saying a different word or phrase other than what you are reading – another useful exercise that you can engage in to minimize sub-vocalization is for you to use a word, phrase, or anything that you can say in your mind other than the words in the material that you're reading. You may be saying something different in your mind, but you'll be surprised that your eyes can recognize the words on the page and even understand them even if you don't sub-vocalize. Try to count while you read the material (say, you count from 1 to 100 while you read this section), and you can see that this phenomenon can be utilized to increase your reading speed.

- Visualize and think about the word, rather than pronouncing it in your head – reading involves thinking, as this is what makes comprehension possible. Hence, rather than thinking of pronouncing the word or phrases, why not just visualize it instead? This will make your mind think more about the material and what it means. Telling your mind to stop sub-vocalizing is not helpful, as it only becomes conscious of its tendency to sub-vocalize rather than process the meaning of the words that you're reading.

- If you're the type who says the words that you're reading using your mouth, what you can do is to keep your mouth occupied. You may deliberately close your mouth and prevent it from opening, or you may chew gum just to prevent yourself from saying a word.

- Develop your vocabulary – most people who adopt this practice experience difficulty understanding the words written in the material (primarily for words that you've encountered for the first time). One way of stopping yourself from sub-vocalizing is to at least have a good vocabulary. You can start reading dictionaries or read a lot of materials. This is where you'll encounter different words, and reading them can help develop your vocabulary. So when you encounter these words, you can easily understand them and continue reading rather than spending time just to decode the meaning of that word. Pre-reading can also be useful to help you develop your vocabulary, as you get to be familiar with the word that needs more attention and research for its meaning early on. This then contributes to prior understanding of these difficult words and makes reading easier for you once you start reading the material for the purpose of extracting information from it.

- Learn to focus on important words – it can be difficult to minimize sub-vocalization when you're just beginning to change this habit. If you want to read faster, you can try to see which words are important and will give you the idea contained in the sentence and limit yourself to pronouncing these words only. Consider the example "Ella is working at a fast food chain so that she can pay her tuition fees". You will read all the words, but will only pronounce those that really convey the meaning of the sentence (in this sentence, those are the words Ella, working, fast food chain, pay tuition fees). These words are enough to help you remember the meaning, increase comprehension, and minimize the number of words that you have to say in your mind.

- Ask questions while you read – when you start to visualize what you're reading and see what it looks like in an actual situation, you can further enhance comprehension by asking questions related to the material.

By doing so, your mind becomes more active in looking for possible answers that may be contained in the material or conceive of ideas that might answer the question. This practice can take away your urge to pronounce the word (as the mind is more occupied with the visualization and seeking the answer).

You cannot totally eliminate the practice of sub-vocalization. After all, there are times when doing so can be helpful in your learning process. However, it is without a doubt that saying each word that you read can greatly inhibit the number of words that you can recognize and understand. By following the guidelines stated above, you can free yourself from a large burden that has been holding down your reading speed.

Chapter 6 – Limiting regression with the use of hand motions

Another practice of most readers that also inhibits their reading speed is re-reading, or what can also be called regression. In this chapter, we will explain why most people engage in this practice. We will also enumerate the methods that can be used to minimize regression. And lastly, we will give a detailed discussion on hand motions and how each of these motions can be executed properly.

Why do people engage in regression?

It was mentioned in the chapter introduction what regression is all about. But despite the obvious fact that it significantly reduces the reading speed of almost anyone, many still continue to engage in it. Here are some of the possible explanations as to its widespread practice:

- The material is not understood sufficiently – when we encounter something in the reading material that we do not fully understand, we have a large tendency to revisit the areas that we've previously read; this is done in the hopes of understanding the concept better before we move on to the next material. After all, there is a large tendency to think that what we've encountered at that moment might be encountered again in the future – and we wouldn't want to go all the way back just to clarify it. Hence, we take the risk of spending more time to understand that single concept. However, regression not only slows down your reading speed; it also inhibits your brain's ability to process information at a much faster rate (since you'll be relying on regression to clarify confusing concepts).

- Something important might be missed – most people think that they might have forgotten important concepts while reading, leading them to re-read the material. However, not everything in the material is important. Some passages are just introductions, anecdotes, or materials that are not very important in explaining the concept. The fact that you don't remember these materials simply means that they are not as important as those that are retained in your mind.

Methods to reduce regression

Here are some of the common methods that you can use to reduce the occurrence of regression while reading.

- Using index cards or non-transparent ruler – if you have developed the habit of looking back at what you've read, it will be hard to get away from it if the "temptation" is present. Hence, it is obvious that what you need to do is to make it physically impossible for you to go back. This can be done by using an index card or non-transparent ruler to cover up the material that you have read.

- Using a pointer – another method to inhibit the tendency to go back to previously read material is to use a pointer such as a pen or your finger. This is because a person's attention is involuntarily captured by any form of movement. The moving pointer also forces the brain and the eyes to follow it; this in turn enables the person to read as many words or ideas as they can in a short amount of time as compared to just focusing on a single or a few words.

Hand motions

Using a pointer is not enough; it has to be combined with hand motions for it to be effective. This section will give a detailed discussion of each hand motion that you can use, along with how each of these hand motions can be done properly.

The starting position

All hand motions should assume a starting position, which can be accomplished by following these steps:

1. Begin by placing your hand (either left or right) on the page. Your palm should be facing towards the page, and your thumb should be placed close to your palm (or under it).

2. Keep your hands and fingers relaxed on the page. Also, your remaining fingers should be slightly apart from one another.

Always make sure that your hand looks like this when you start reading.

Underlining movement

This is the most basic among all hand motions, and it is recommended for people who are just beginning to learn how to speed read.

Here is the step-by-step guide to doing this hand motion:

1. With your hand in the starting position,

smoothly and steadily run your hand on the material to be read, similar to underlining the words in each line. Maintain your focus on where the finger is pointing.

2. Once you reach the last word in the line, slightly raise your finger and bring it on the next line by moving your hand diagonally.

3. Repeat steps 1 and 2 until you reach the last line of the page.

Once you get used to reading with the aid of this hand motion, you can then use other hand motions for faster reading.

S-hand movement

This hand motion is similar to the underlining movement, although with some changes. In this hand motion, you do not lift your hand when shifting to the next line. Also, you have the option to do either a tight "S" movement (aims to run through each line in the page and read the words at a much faster rate) or a wide "S" movement (more useful for previewing the contents of the page).

Here is a step-by-step guide on how to execute the tight "S" movement:

1. Follow the starting position and place it on

the second line of the page.

2. Mimic the motion of a reverse S (starting from the left to the right) until it reaches the end of that line.

3. Once you reach the end of the line, move your hand on the bottom of the third line where your finger was once placed (your finger should be on the right side of the page by this time). Continue running your finger on that line until it reaches the left side of the page.

4. Continue the motion until you're finished with the page.

If you want to do the wide "S" movement, you only need to make a large S on the page. It should still start on the left side of the page though.

With the S hand movement, you are forced to recognize as many words as you can while keeping up with the motion. This is because unlike in the underlining movement, your hand skips on certain lines. This will teach you how to recognize and understand the words horizontally and vertically.

X-hand movement

This is another hand movement that mimics the motion in writing the letter. It is advised that only those who have been practicing speed reading for quite some time should use this hand movement. This hand motion involves angular movement, and is mostly used for materials that are written in columns such as newspaper articles.

Here is a step-by-step guide on how this hand motion can be properly executed.

1. Assuming the starting position, place your hand on the first word of the page. From the starting point, move your index finger diagonally, going to the other side of the page. Your end point should be four or five lines below your starting point.

2. Switch from the index to the middle finger, and make an angular movement going to the second line of the page (still on the right side).

3. Once your finger is on the second line, move diagonally going to the left side of the page. Move through the same number of lines stated in step 1.

4. Upon reaching the left side, switch back to using your index finger as the pointer when you move upward. Repeat the previous steps until you're finished with the page and all of the material.

This hand motion involves the switching between

the index and middle fingers. The switch reduces the friction experienced by your fingers as compared to just using a single finger to run through the material. This motion is also helpful in developing diagonal eye movement while your peripheral vision is used. You also learn to recognize words in advance, and make sense of all that you've seen even if you don't read them in the order that the author has intended.

Loop hand movement

This hand motion is considered as a variation to the X-hand movement. This is because both of these hand motions use diagonal movement. However, this motion is different in the way that it uses curves rather than angles. This method appeals to people who do not want to shift fingers while doing the hand motion. The benefit of using this hand motion is the same as when you use the X-hand movement.

Here are the steps that should be followed to properly execute this hand motion.

1. Your finger (either the index or the middle finger) should be on the first word on the page.

2. Make a diagonal movement going to the right side of the page. Your end point should be on the fourth or fifth line after your starting point.

3. Move upward to the second line. But instead of making an angle, make a sharp curve going to the target line; the movement should be similar to doing an infinity symbol (∞).

4. From the 2nd line on the right side of the page, repeat the same motion and follow the same number of lines when you move your finger to the other side of the page.

5. Repeat the steps until you've finished going through the page and the whole material.

L-hand movement

When you combine the underlining, loop, and X hand motions, you can come up with this hand movement. Although it is mostly useful for reading materials presented in columns, it can also be used when you want to preview the material.

This hand motion can be properly executed by following these steps:

1. Assuming the starting position, place your hand on the third line of the left side of the page.

2. Move through the line where your finger is located, similar to doing the underlining movement.

3. Once you've reached the right side of that line, move your finger up to the second line that preceded your starting point.

4. From that position, move your finger diagonally going to the left side of the page. Your end point should be the fifth line from where you started the diagonal movement.

5. Once you reach the left side, make a curving motion going two lines up from where the diagonal movement ended.

6. Repeat step 2 on this line, then repeat the procedures until you've finished with the page and the material.

Using the underlining motion along with the other motions allows you to focus on some of the lines in the material as opposed to using the X or Loop hand movement alone.

Question mark movement

If your purpose is to preview the important points in the material, the question mark hand motion is recommended. This is a much faster hand motion as compared to the hand motions that were previously presented. It can also be used if you want to train your eyes and brain to recognize more words in a shorter amount of time.

Here is the step-by-step procedure of this hand motion:

1. Assume the starting position of your hands. Your starting point should be the first word on the page.

2. From this point, trace the figure of a question mark (similar to making a wide S movement).

3. The end point of your hand should be at the center of the last line in the page. Repeat the motion on the next pages.

Aside from training your eyes to recognize as many ideas as possible in that page, you also learn how to read horizontally in both directions. This is because the question mark motion requires you to land on the center-bottom part of the page. It is also necessary to read the last line in any page, as you won't be able to follow the contents of the next page if you don't have an idea about the last concept written on the previous page.

Conclusion

Thank you again for downloading this book!

I hope this book was able to help you to develop your speed reading skills.

Finally, if you enjoyed this book, please take the time to share your thoughts and post a review on Amazon. It'd be greatly appreciated!

Thank you and good luck!

12594917R00035

Made in the USA
San Bernardino, CA
21 June 2014